WHEN THE STARS WERE STILL VISIBLE

poems

Maria Mazziotti Gillan

STEPHEN F. AUSTIN STATE UNIVERSITY PRESS

Production Manager: Kimberly Verhines
Cover Art: "When the Stars Were Still Visible" by Maria Mazziotti Gillan

IBSN: 978-1-62288-913-6

For more information:
Stephen F. Austin State University Press
P.O. Box 13007 SFA Station
Nacogdoches, Texas 75962
sfapress@sfasu.edu
www.sfasu.edu/sfapress
936-468-1078

Distributed by Texas A&M University Press Consortium
www.tamupress.com

Other Books by Maria Mazziotti Gillan

Flowers from the Tree of Night, Chantry Press, 1980

Winter Light, Chantry Press, 1985

Luce D'Inverno, Cross-Cultural Communications, 1987

The Weather of Old Seasons, Cross-Cultural Communications, 1987

Taking Back My Name, Malafemmina Press, 1990; Lincoln Springs Press, 1991, repeated printings

Where I Come From: Selected and New Poems, Guernica Editions, 1995, 1997

Things My Mother Told Me, Guernica Editions, 1999

Italian Women in Black Dresses, Guernica Editions, 2002, 2003, 2004

Maria Mazziotti Gillan: Greatest Hits 1972-2002, Pudding House Publications, 2003

Talismans/Talismani, Ibiskos Editions, 2006

All That Lies Between Us, Guernica Editions, 2006

Nightwatch, Poems by Maria Mazziotti Gillan and Aeronwy Thomas, The Seventh Quarry Press, 2010

Moments in the Past That Shine, The Ridgeway Press, 2010

What We Pass On: Collected Poems: 1980-2009, Guernica Editions, 2010

The Place I Call Home, NYQ Books, 2012

Writing Poetry to Save Your Life: How to Find the Courage to Tell Your Stories, MiroLand, Guernica, 2013

The Silence in the Empty House, NYQ Books, 2013

Ancestors' Song, Bordighera Press, 2013

The Girls in the Chartreuse Jackets, Cat in the Sun Books, 2014

In a Place of Flowers and Light: San Mauro and MIa Mama, a cura di Osvaldo Marrocco, 2014

Women Who Are Afraid of Nothing: Storia Del Passato Perduto E Mai Piu Ritrovato, a cura di Osvaldo Marrocco, translated from English to Italian by Maria Giovanna Barra, 2016

What Blooms in Winter, NYQ Books, 2016

Paterson Light and Shadow with photographs by Mark Hillringhouse, Serving House Books, 2017

for Linda Hillringhouse
and the painting poets' camp

Table of Contents

When the Stars Were Still Visible

In the photo, I am on the back steps of the six-family tenement
on 5th Avenue in Paterson where I was born.
I am squinting into the sun,
my nose wrinkled, my eyes closed against the glare.
I am two years old, my hair a curly cap on my head.
It looks blonde, though I know it couldn't have been,
and wonder if I am remembering my daughter at two,
sitting in the little rocking chair on the front porch
on Oak Street in Kansas City. Her hair was all blonde ringlets.

Strange how memory is like the fragments of a puzzle:
Remember the green blackout shades in our apartment
in Paterson in 1944.

Remember my father dressed as a devil for a costume party
at the Società Cilentana on Butler Street.

Remember the silver ball Zio Guillermo made
from the foil inside the Camel cigarettes he smoked
that stained his fingers yellow.

So many memories swirl
like bits of color in a kaleidoscope,
and so impossible to explain.

Remember 17th Street with Mrs. Gianelli
who always fainted when she got upset
and the old man who ran the candy store
that was so filthy no one bought anything there,
and the big garage in the Gianelli's backyard

where we put on plays until something happened;
I don't know what, something to do with playing doctor
behind our improvised curtains
and then we weren't allowed to play there anymore.

Remember Zio Guillermo's garden
with tomatoes and zucchini and corn,
and the vacant lot next door that seemed so huge,
you'd think we had all of New Jersey to play in,
until I see it years later,
covered with asphalt and garages
and I realize that the entire block,
my world until I was eleven, wasn't that big
and certainly the lot, small, and now so ugly.

Remember Paterson when the stars were still visible in the sky
and I didn't know 17th Street was in a city.

Remember the sweet smell of marigolds and daisies in the vacant lot,
and our house full of food and laughter,
our family together under the kitchen light,
the company of honorary aunts and uncles.
Outside, our friends gathered to play stickball in the street,
hours to fill with games and books and dreaming.
How lucky I was, how lucky,
Paterson glowing and sparkling
like a silver ball in my hands.

The Children of Immigrants

The children of immigrants don't know their ancestors
except through blue airmail letters—
my father's mother, my mother's mother.
They are vague outlines that will never be filled in
except in a photograph.
They are all dressed in black, always in mourning,
so they had to wear black for a year or two
even if they were young women,
black through hot Italian summers, even black stockings.
My mother's mother was thin and frail looking
with a sweet face. My father's mother was sturdy
and full faced, her long thick hair pulled back
in a knot at the back of her head. She was not smiling.
We have another picture of her,
a studio photograph in a mahogany frame
where she is posed next to my grandfather.
They do not touch. She is wearing a black dress
with a small lace collar. He is dressed in a black suit,
a shirt with a stiff, starched collar, dark tie.
They are both staring into the camera.

At ninety-two, my father told me his father had deserted
my grandmother and their children when she was twenty-four,
that he had gone to Argentina and had never come back.
My grandmother's face had revealed nothing.
Pride had kept her head held high in that mountain village
where everyone knew her husband had forgotten her,
where she had to support her children by doing find needle work
while the priest's housekeeper brought them food from the rectory.

Children of immigrants pick up bits and pieces
over the years to create a picture.

My father had tried to protect his sisters
from my grandmother's rage. She would beat them,
his sisters who were all six feet tall.
My five-foot-three-inch father would step
between his mother and sisters
and he would end up tied to the bed.

My father was blessed with a forgiving nature—
he never was angry with my grandmother.
My father wrote to her often,
sent packages of food and clothes
that my mother would wrap in white cloth,
then sew together and seal the edges with red sealing wax,
so no one at the post office could open the package
before it reached my grandmother.

We also heard my grandfather had a new wife in Argentina.
What part of these women might also be a part of me, part of my children?
What did they love? How much had they cried
when their own children left home for America
and they never saw them again?

Carrying Their Hometowns to Paterson

On the street where I grew up,
everyone knew everyone else.
We knew each other's secrets,
though we pretended we didn't.
Our street was lined with
two- and three-family houses
full of immigrants from southern Italy.
There was one young Irish couple
. . . they moved out quickly.
Another Italian family moved in.
These immigrants came from Cilento
and Calabria and Sicily. Paterson, at the time,
had fifty Italian societies,
named for different Italian regions and towns.
My father belonged to the Cilentano society
where he went to play cards
and argue about politics with the other men.
The members of the ladies auxiliary cooked
spaghetti dinners for the men
at least once a month. On our street
it was as though these new immigrants
carried their hometowns to Paterson,
carrying their dialects and mores
and the pungent cheeses their relatives sent to them
so they'd have a piece of home
to remind them of the past.
On summer evenings they would sit around
oilcloth-covered tables under the grape arbors
they had planted, playing cards and talking.

They needed their countrymen to replace the relatives
they had left behind in those Italian villages,

those people they never saw again.
They worked hard in America where the streets
were not paved in gold, but where they knew
they could give their children better lives
than what they could have given them
if they'd stayed in the mountain villages
they called home.

The Face We Presented to the World

I come from a cold-water flat heated by a coal stove
where my mother cooked and baked and near which we sat
to play games like Monopoly or checkers, or to do our homework.
My mother wanted us to be close and we always were.
I am from a metal espresso pot with a black handle and homemade bread
and HO Cream Farina and milk with Bosco in it.

I'm from five-and-dime-store cups and dishes, plain and ugly.
I'm from the back stoop where we sat with our friends on summer evenings,
smoking punks and catching fireflies in Mason jars with little holes
     punched in the lids.

I'm from the place where everyone used the back door when they visited,
even the milkman and the Fuller Brush salesman
and all the aunts, uncles, cousins and honorary relatives.

I'm from a place where Italian dialect was spoken,
and from political arguments and laughter.

I'm from an oilcloth-covered table,
my mother's homemade macaroni
and from everything else made from scratch.

I am from dish towels made from flour sacks,
hand-me-down clothes and *bella figura*,
my mother believing that if you were leaving the house
your clothes needed to be clean and neat and starched,
hair washed and combed, face shining,
the face we presented to the world
scrubbed clear of worry
so we would make a good impression
and didn't have to be ashamed.

Growing Up in My Mother's House

Growing up in my mother's house meant the aroma
of baked bread and soup, *pasta fagoli* or lentils and chicken,
meatballs and gravy and homemade macaroni,
meant Monopoly and gin rummy
with my brother and sister after supper in the big kitchen
on 17th Street in Paterson, meant sitting on a kitchen chair
and reading on the front stoop.

Growing up in my mother's house meant not knowing
we were poor, no TV until I was eleven, visits
to my aunts and uncles, who all lived close.
Even though there was barely enough money
for food for us, my mother found a way to stretch it,
ways to include everyone who came by,
"Pull up a chair," she'd say,
and another person would join us,
the family large and elastic
and always ready to include one more.

My mother's house meant an icebox and the iceman
lifting the block of ice with his tongs, meant milk
and butter delivered at the back door by the men
from Lakeview Dairy, meant a garden rich with vegetables
and spices that my mother grew and gathered to use
in the food she cooked for us, everything served on 5 & 10 cent
stone crockery, everything perfectly cooked and seasoned.
"The food must look good," my mother said. "The colors need
to complement one another." Six or seven different dishes
on the table at once, followed by fruit and walnuts

and lemon cake and espresso, all of us together,
moments in that house so clear to me
though that 17th Street kitchen was more than fifty years ago,
I can still smell those meals,
still see my mother in her homemade apron
walking between the coal stove and the table.

Lace Curtains

My mother had imitation lace curtains—
all the immigrant women in Riverside
had the same curtains.
My mother washed them by hand in the kitchen sink,
used curtain stretchers to dry them.
The stretchers were large rectangles of wood
with small nails sticking out of them
so the curtains could be pulled tight across the frame.
When they were dry, my mother would lift them off the nails
and hang them on the windows.
We, with our washers and dryers and cleaning ladies,
can't imagine the amount of time
the women of my childhood spent cleaning and washing,
all the time it took to wash each item by hand,
the time to stretch curtains before hanging them.
My mother worked in factories in Paterson,
but she still rose each day at 4 a.m.
to bake bread and get dinner ready for the evening.
In all that time as a child, I never heard my mother complain,
never heard regret in her voice, or shame, or rage.
She was always the stone platform on which we stood.

And only in the evening after dinner,
after washing dishes, after ironing clothes,
my mother would sit in the rocker
with the coal stove pumping heat
into the room, and tell stories in Italian,
her voice the stream we floated on
as we sailed toward sleep.

Motion Sickness

When I was a child, I threw up a lot. Every time
I climbed into the back seat of a car, I knew
about five minutes before it would happen.
We didn't have a car of our own,
so it was usually in my cousin Joey's car.
Joey came to hate me, though he never said.
I was so ashamed that I finally learned
to speak up, to ask him to stop,
so I could be sick at the side of the road.

When I was about seven, my mother and I
went to church to watch Julio get married.
Julio who'd say, "Will you marry me? I'll wait for you."
On the way out of Blessed Sacrament Church
on 16th Street in Paterson, I threw up
on Mrs. Gianelli's fur coat.

Mrs. Gianelli was delicate, blonde and lovely.
Her husband treated her like a queen.
She had some psychological condition
that caused her to faint whenever she got upset.
This time, she managed to click
her high heels out of the church,
but surely, she must have fainted
when she got home.

The Paper Dolls of My Childhood

The paper dolls of my childhood
came inside books.
They had perforations
so they could be removed
and the clothes had them too, with little tags on them
so they could be folded over
on the paper doll.

The dolls themselves
were flat and made of card stock,
material strong enough
to hold the dresses and skirts and coats
we attached to them, pretending
such an immense wardrobe was possible
though our own closets
held only two outfits for school
and one Sunday dress.
My sister and I had a tiny room, so we shared the small closet.
My mother washed and ironed a lot,
the apartment filled with the aroma
of starch that was dissolved in water and sprinkled on
       clothes.
The iron was literally iron and heated on a coal stove.

The paper dolls of my childhood were thick and one-dimensional.
They bring back a time when I could play by myself
for hours, sitting on the linoleum and making up stories
and places for those dolls to go, outfits for them to wear.

My daughter, when she was growing up, had Barbie dolls
which were a 1970s replacement for paper dolls

but much more expensive and elaborate.
Barbie also had a "Barbie dream house"
and "Barbie sports car" and "Barbie beach house,"
things I could not have imagined
while I sat int he living room and played with the paper dolls.
I realize now that both kinds of dolls made us dream
of all the things we wanted to have,
all the things we thought we would get
in the sparkling future we were sure waited for us.

They made us believe that if we had the right house,
the right clothes, the right car, we would be happy.

For my daughter, I wanted a life filled with everything
I never could've had.
I was a young mother and I didn't understand
how all the things we held in our hands,
all the things we could not buy,
are not the things that transform us,
not the things that fill us with light
like the new moon that loomed over the sky the other night,
the one that only appears once in seventy years,
so when it does

ah, the magic that a moon can be so beautiful and rare,
we can barely keep ourselves rooted to the ground.

Looking Back, I See Myself in Third Grade

Looking back, I see myself in third grade
dreamy, shy, a child afraid of everything,
always afraid that I'd make a mistake,
speaking Italian instead of English,
my long thin face, my sausage curls,
my huge dark eyes.
I tried to hide
by folding my hands neatly on my desk,
by looking down at the names carved on its surface by
generations of other children.

Third grade,
where teachers began to read poems and stories to us,
where I fell in love with the sound of English read aloud,
me, in my neatly ironed hand-me-down dresses,
me, with my olive-toned skin listening to Longfellow
or John Greenleaf Whittier
or Edgar Arlington Robinson
read by the teacher in unaccented English,
the language so beautiful, their poems carrying me away
from the dusty time-worn classroom
to a place where words could sing in my head.
At the end of each day, I could go home
to a place where I could forget to be afraid.

I was happy to go back to my mother's kitchen
where I could eat homemade bread fresh out of the oven,
home to the aroma of herbs—basil and rosemary and oregano
wafting through the house,
and greeting me like a kiss each day at the door.

Taking My Brother to the Barber

When we were children, my mother assigned each of us
to a younger child, so I was supposed to look after
my younger brother when he needed a haircut. He was seven and I was ten.
I walked him up to Lorenzo's barbershop
on Fifth Avenue and 17th Street.
The shop was at the top of a steep hill,
and we would climb, Alex and I,
to the shop with the swirled barber's pole,
red and white and sharply visible
in my memory; it was all almost seventy years ago.

At my sister's funeral, someone came up to me and said,
"I can still see you and Alessandro.
You'd walk with him and you'd be wagging your finger
and telling him what to do,"
and he would listen
with that centered stillness he possessed,
and that he still has now,
though he's been a doctor for more than nearly fifty years.

The barber, Lorenzo,
would place a booster seat across the arms of a large barber's chair
and pick my brother up and put him on it.
He'd always cut his hair the same way
as if he'd placed an imaginary bowl on it.
Then he'd put powder on his face with a big brush
to remove any stray hairs that had fallen.
We'd walk out of the shop and return home,
down that hill and in the back door of the flat.

My brother is my doctor now; he is seventy-five and not seven,
but some of that little boy I dragged up 17th Street is still there
and his face still has that same calm, soothing demeanor.
Now, I am the one asking him what I should do,
what medicine to take. Though I've seen many other specialists,
he is the only doctor I really trust.
He never says that I should lose weight though I know that I should,
or that I should do more exercise.
Instead, he offers comfort
and solace and just the right prescription for me
after some specialist decides I should have some complex
and dangerous procedure and then says, *I have to tell you,*
the procedure could leave you paralyzed or give you a stroke.
My brother always says, "No, I wouldn't do that,
too risky and not enough chance that it will succeed."
He reassures me, "Better to be cautious. Surgery is a last resort,"
and suddenly I see him as a little boy, so serious, so self-contained
even when I'd acted like a big boss who scolded him
and he would turn those huge dark eyes on me
and never complain.

Ode to the Movie Theaters of My Childhood

We would take the bus from the Riverside section of Paterson
downtown to go to the movies on Saturdays
—my mother forced my older sister to take me with her and her friends—
and we would go to the Fabian theater or the Rivoli.
They were all elegant,
red velvet draperies on the walls,
cherubs carved into the ceiling rosettes,
the plush velvet seats.
It was the late 1940s, after the war
and Paterson was still thriving.

I mourn the loss of these theaters,
too many sitting in disrepair
like the Fabian that bears no resemblance
to what it looked like so many years ago.
Some of these elegant theaters
have been partitioned into smaller theaters,
so that four or five movies
can be shown at the same time.
I miss those big theaters, that velvety elegance,
all those old movies with their wealthy characters,
women in long evening gowns and cigarette holders,
men in tuxedos and top hats, fancy cars with chauffeurs,
and once the lights were dimmed and the music started
we were transported to places we had never been
or had little hope of ever seeing.
But those movies made us a part of those characters' lives,
made us imagine that one day, we too, could go to the Biltmore or Sardi's.
The lights would come back on after the movies ended.
We would sit for a moment in our seats
before we returned to our ordinary lives.

My Sister Was Afraid of Thunder

I see myself standing behind the door
of the 19th Street tenement.
I am eleven years old.
My sister stands next to me. She is fifteen
and although she looks like a dark-haired Marilyn Monroe,
she is shaking and furious.
See, she yells, *you did this.*
Now we're going to die in a thunderstorm
and it's all your fault.
I am skinny, shy, and inarticulate.
I feel guilty though some part of me knows
I had nothing to do with bringing these bolts of lightning,
these huge gongs of thunder.
Over the years I came to understand
that my sister had an irrational fear of thunder,
though she was very bright, especially in science,
and very practical and efficient in every other way but this one.
Years later, she would pass this fear onto her daughter, Annamaria,
who eventually would babysit my children.
My son still tells stories about her.
If it thundered, she wanted my children to hide in the closet,
and even as a child, my son thought it was funny.
He'd say, "What is that I hear, Annamaria? Go hide," and she would.
Now my son is fifty-two years old. Annamaria is fifty-six and confined
    to her bed
with advanced MS. She has two children who are teenagers
and help to take care of her.
Every few days, she calls me to describe the latest disaster—
legs that cannot move,
a bedsore so deep it is hitting bone.

I hear her trembling through the phone.
I can't stand the pain anymore, she says,
I can't even sit in my chair.
This is no life, she tells me.
I think about Annamaria and her fear of thunder.
I wonder if she ever imagined her life would end like this,
a disease so terrible that the fear of thunder must seem like a kindness.

I Was the Good Girl

I was the good girl,
the quiet, bookish girl, the one who tried
to hide because she was terrified
of the teachers who had their eyes on her.

I was the good girl, hands hidden
in my desk, too shy to speak,
too shy to ask to be counted.
If I were quiet enough, I thought,
no one would notice I was there.

I was the good girl, my thin skin
easily wounded by cruelty or shame,
the girl who sat in the seventh-grade classroom
at PS 18, Mr. Landgraff
and Mrs. Richmond talking about me.
"Look at her," they'd say.
"Such a shy little rabbit. I bet
her father beats her,"

and I withdrew into the center of myself,
trying not to know that they had spoken loud enough
for everyone in the class to hear.
The clock ticked slowly, like an axe chopping off
seconds until the 3 p.m. bell

when I could escape to my tiny room to cry
and bury my shame in a place so deep
I could pretend to myself
it was not there.

In Grammar School

In grammar school, in the dusty
classroom of PS 18, I sit at the scarred
wooden desks and I wait
for what will happen, certain
that nothing good will come to me.
On the playground, the athletic girls jump rope
Double-Dutch, while I watch, klutzy even then,
and knowing it is futile even to try.

In grammar school, I am the class mascot—
not part of a clique, but so wide-eyed
and innocent, all the other kids make it
their duty to protect me, though when
they exchange friendship rings, I have only
one friend to give one to me.

In seventh grade, the girls separate
into the ones who will attract boys
and the ones who will never be blessed
and beautiful. The popular girls believe
they are popular because they deserve to be,
the rest of us watch, too distant
from them to feel jealous, know that unless
fairy godmothers pop out of a story,
nothing will make us know
how it is to be born in the skin
of the girls who are chosen,
the ones invited to all parties, the ones
who will be first to wear a boy's ring
on a chain around their necks.

Once we were all invited to a party and the girls
were supposed to come to my house to pick me up,
but I waited and waited, and no one came.
The next day, I lied, said I was sick, and that's why
I didn't go to the party, ashamed to admit
that the girls had forgotten all about me,
so invisible was I, so unimportant,
that the others didn't even know
they had left me behind.

The Popular Girls in Seventh Grade

formed a club, called the Ritz Girls.
There were three of them,
the prettiest girls in the class,
the ones all the boys liked.
They seemed to be born knowing
how to speak to boys.
Judy, Diane and Andrea, the Ritz Girls,
held their meetings in Andrea's basement
in her Dutch colonial house at the top of 19th Street hill.
They exchanged friendship rings and whispered in corners
of the classroom and made plans to wear
color-coordinated sweaters on certain days.
I watched them, the circle they created,
that seemed sprinkled with pixie dust.
Judy was my first friend because she lived on the same street,
and we played together in the lower grades.
But by sixth grade, it was obvious
I would never be one of the popular girls—
I never knew what to say to boys
or how to make them look at me
the way they looked at the Ritz Girls.

Andrea got married right after high school.
Judy married the boy she met on the bus to Benedictine Academy.
While they were still in high school,
he would beat her up and even broke her arm.
Years later, I heard that she had gained a lot of weight
and her husband was often violent. They had four children.
The last time he beat her so severely,
he broke her jaw and her eye socket.

She spent three weeks in the hospital.
Finally, she filed for a divorce.
Diane moved out of town and later became a nurse.
I never saw her again.

But I remember the three of them
because they seemed destined in seventh grade for magical lives.
The Ritz Girls, although they were part of my life so long ago,
I will never forget how they seemed so exquisite and perfect.
And I know now that as we live our lives,
magic never lasts.

Eighth Grade Kiss

My first kiss was in eighth grade at Andrea Correa's party
when Nick Rossi pulled me into an armchair with him
and clamped his lips to my mouth so we looked like
those kissing dolls, the ones with magnets in their lips.
Over Nick's shoulder I saw Andrea kissing Joe Clemente,
her arms around his neck, her leg lifted
the way movie stars and comic book heroines kissed,
that leg—Andrea's attempt at sophistication.
I wanted desperately to feel something with Nick's lips clamped to mine.
I wanted to be passionate like the heroines of the romance novels I loved,
but nothing happened, not for me,
except I couldn't wait for it to end,
the party,
the endless kiss
and poor Nick, who I realized didn't feel anything either,
as bored and desperate as I was,
both of us wanting to be part of the crowd,
wanting to be grown up and sexy
even though we both just wanted to go home.

The Boys I Loved, the Boys Who Loved Me

In second grade, I loved Herman Westfall,
because I was worried that Miss Elmer hated him.
She hit poor, fidgety Herman
across the knuckles with the ruler.
He sat next to me. I was always scared
she was planning to bring
that ruler down on my own knuckles.

In seventh grade, I loved a boy
whose name I cannot remember.
He lived next door and used to walk home
with me from <u>PS 18</u> in Paterson. He was beautiful,
so blond and blue-eyed, so American.
His father was always drunk and beat him
with a razor strap. I pretended I didn't know.

At thirteen, Big Joey loved me, but I was too naïve
to understand. At his birthday party, he led me
to his bedroom and kissed me. I was so surprised,
I fell backward onto his bed. He ran away,
both of us embarrassed.
One day, in the cafeteria at East Side High School,
he gave me a book, called *India Allen*.
"Here," he said, thrusting the book into my hand.
I didn't understand what he was trying to say.

At seventeen, I loved a boy who was Mr. Popularity in high school,
one of the few blond-haired, blue-eyed Italians I knew.
He was on the baseball team, was tall and athletic.
He had a beautiful girlfriend. He thought I was

innocent and sweet. He wanted me to be her friend.

So much I didn't understand and sometimes
I think I lived inside a dream,
didn't get any of the clues everyone else
seemed to get without trying.

At Thirteen, They Still Called Us Girls

They used to call us girls when I was in high school.
We were not offended.
We knew we weren't women yet,
saw too often in our own neighborhood
what being a woman meant,
so we were happy to exist in that country
caught between childhood and grown-up life.
After school at East Side High School, we'd walk downtown
to parade up and down Main Street in Paterson.
We didn't have money, so we'd pass by
the beautiful displays in Meyer Brothers' windows,
too intimidated to walk the perfumed aisles
of a fancy department store.
The only places we weren't afraid to go
were the 5 & 10 cent stores—Woolworth's or WT Grant.
We'd walk up and down those aisles checking out
lipstick colors and nail polish,
inexpensive bangles, imitation leather purses.

Woolworth's had a long counter with glass bins
that held an assortment of candies, replicas of M&M's,
Good & Plenty, or gummy candies.
Sometimes, my mother would go downtown
and bring back a small, clear plastic container of candy
and we'd eat them one or two at a time,
knowing they'd have to last.
In our house, my mother made everything from scratch,
so store-bought candy was an exquisite pleasure.
When we emptied the box, we'd use it as doll furniture.

They still called us girls then. We'd walk up
and down Main Street for a few hours
and then we'd take separate buses back home.
In my memory, Main Street is always sun lit,
always a perfect autumn day, always alive
with shoppers carrying bags with cord handles.
We didn't have to buy anything to enjoy walking on Main,
our minds full of dreams, the hope on our faces,
full of all that glittered and sparkled
in the air around us.

I've Always Envied Women with Beautiful Hair

I've always envied women with beautiful hair,
long, straight hair that's thick and lustrous,
flowing sensually when they moved.
I had thick kinky hair. Since we were poor,
my mother took me to a hairdresser
who had her "shoppe" in the living room of her house.
She insisted on thinning my hair with the special scissors.
They were designed to cut out every second or third hair
and when she was finished,
she'd shape it into a triangle around my thin face
so my hair looked like a tent
framing my big eyes,
my big nose.

I read *Seventeen* magazine,
wanted straight blonde hair shaped into a page boy,
wanted to look like the upper-middle-class girls
featured in those pages,
their wealth and privilege evident
in their perfect haircuts,
the preppy clothes.
No wonder in the pictures of me from that time,
I always have my head bent,
my eyes lowered,
my shoulders hunched
as though I would be able to hide what I was,
what I thought I would always be.

East Side High School, Paterson, NJ

When I think of high school,
that place where I tried too hard to fit in but never did,
that place where I only made two new friends in the four years I was there,
that place jammed full of so many other people I didn't know,
the halls full of rushing students in bobby socks,
the steel lockers that lined the halls,
I remember the taste of fear mingled with loneliness,
the way I was sure everyone else knew a secret I could never learn,
that crowded and noisy cafeteria where my neighbor, Big Joey,
handed me a romance novel called *India Allen*,
that place where Mr. Weiss, my English teacher,
treated me as though I were special.
I was hungry for the courage he handed me,
quiet, skinny, and awkward in my gray wool skirt and saddle shoes,
my head always bent, my shoulders hunched.
Now years later, when I give a poetry reading in New York City,
Mr. Weiss often attends and sits near the front.
When I see him, I feel as though I grow taller, surer.
How grateful I am to see him there, smiling at me and nodding.

One time after reading my poems in Chicago,
a man approached me. "Hi," he said, "I'm Joey. Remember me?"
He and his wife gave me a personal tour of Chicago, took me out to eat.
We had lunch at a diner where the waitresses danced on the counters
and Joey had two cheeseburgers and French fries,
though he had just had open heart surgery. Joey wasn't that healthy.
He had been married three times and his wife was years younger than he.
She adored him. Joey liked to have a good time,
wasn't good at doling out pleasures one at a time.

Last year, my brother called up to say Joey had died,
Joey, this remnant of my childhood,
who shoved a book in my hands in the Eastside High School cafeteria
because he loved me.

Frank Sinatra's Voice on the Jukebox

sings "My Funny Valentine"
in the basement Student Union at Seton Hall University.
I am seventeen, naïve, awkward, unsure.
I have a crush on Joey K. who is 5 foot 10 and skinny, all knees and
elbows.
Joey K. is energy and motion and Joey is as naïve as I am.
We both edit the school newspaper.
I really like it, not because I like journalism,
but because it gives me a chance to spend time with Joey in the school
newspaper office.
The editing gives us something to talk about,
relieves the awkward tension between us.
I love his thatch of black hair,
his eyes, small and round as shoe buttons,
his black horned-rimmed glasses.
I am attracted to him because he looks so fragile.
Freshman year he takes me to the Christmas dance.
Did I ask him or did he ask me?
I buy a dress, cherry red and fitted at the bodice but with a flared skirt.

We drive to the dance in Bobby T.'s father's Buick, the size of a boat.
Joey and I sit in the backseat.
He does not touch me. I do not touch him.
He is no one's idea of a valentine
but to me he is *my* funny valentine and the song
fits his awkward movements perfectly,
fits that moment in time,
the big backseat of the car,
Joey's arm finally around me on the way home,
his thin lips press hard against mine.

I was glad he kissed me, but I felt nothing,
except his lips pressing on mine and I didn't know enough
to understand that a kiss should be more than this.
There was no spark at all, but I so needed to be loved,
so needed to have someone's arms around me,
I did not realize that Joey K. was only my funny valentine in my mind,
my heart and body unmoved by him,
yet each time I hear that song I think of him,
and feel a rush of tenderness
for him, for me, for all we didn't know.

The Night I Lost My Virginity

The night I lost my virginity it was snowing.
The soft big flakes covered the ground and the trees
in what seemed like seconds.
Bobby and I had been dating for a year.
We did what people did in the '50s,
parked at Lambert Castle lookout and necked.
We both lived at home so we improvised.
That night, that night
when the snow was falling fast,
we parked at the edge of a construction site.
Bobby took my hand and led me onto the site.
His uncle was the foreman,
so Bobby knew where they kept the key.
He pushed everything off a table that served as a desk
and lifted me up onto that gritty surface where I lost my virginity.
I was disappointed that it wasn't as exciting as I had expected.
I was afraid we'd get caught,
but Bobby was happy he finally talked me into it,
little Catholic girl who wanted to follow all the rules.
Bobby was able to talk me into anything.
I was ashamed that I, in my gray wool skirts,
and broadcloth shirts, and knee socks,
and circle pins, had sex in a place like this,
and from then on anyplace we could,
even in his bedroom when his mother wasn't home
and once on the beach at Long Beach Island.
When we walked into the dunes, Bobby pushed me down
into the beach grass where I was afraid we'd be caught,
Bobby's ass rising and falling above me.
Shame was like a scarf wrapped around my neck

for that year and for a long time after we broke up;
Shame that I still pretended that I was pure and untouched;
Shame that I was so easily won by a few words
and a walk through the snow.

My First Real Boyfriend

My first real boyfriend,
the one I never mentioned
not even to my husband, ever,
the one I still can't think about without flinching,
the one I met at the Literary Club
at Seton Hall in South Orange,
the one who looked nothing like
the blond, blue-eyed men I always fell for,
the one who kept asking me to go out until I finally said yes,
the one who was so persistent
he could talk me into anything, even making love in his car
despite the stick shift and the handbrake
so we had to be contortionists
in order to manage it.
I can still see the steamed-up windows
in his old car that he would park at the T-Bowl Lanes
on Hamburg Turnpike in Wayne.
He'd find a corner far away from the glare of the T-Bowl's neon lights,
and I was always terrified
that the police would arrive
and shine their lights on us.
Each time I'd swear to myself
that I would never do this again but of course, I did.
I can feel the cracked leather
of that old car on my back,
the mixture of excitement and terror,
the inability to stop.
I have erased his name from my memory,
although I know I used to write it hundreds of times
in my notebook.

In Our House Nobody Ever Said

In our house, nobody ever said you're ugly.
My sister was beautiful with her white, white skin,
her full lips, her chocolate brown eyes, her straight teeth.
She is to the right of me in this studio photo
my mother bought from a photographer
who traveled door to door in the Riverside section of Paterson.
My brother is on the left, his wide dark eyes
in his sweet face that looks solemn, self-contained,
as he does now, a doctor for more than forty years.
In the middle, I stare into the camera,
my hair a tangle of black curls,
my lips formed into a shy smile.
I know that I am not beautiful. Even then, I knew it.
I look like I am plugged into an electric socket, energy crackling off me
as though I already have things I need to do and I can't wait.

In our house, we all had our place:
my brother engrossed in encyclopedias my parents bought on time
from a door-to-door salesman,
my sister off to play baseball with the boys on 25th Street,
her body strong and athletic,
and I, who always had a book in my hand, even at the dinner table,
I, who found in books the life I wasn't brave enough to live,
who found in language the beauty that lifted me
out of the constraints of my world.

When I announced at seventeen that I wanted to be a poet,
nobody ever said "You are insane. How will you earn a living?"
Instead, my mother, who sewed the lining in coats in the factories of

Paterson,
saved pennies every week for a year
until she had enough to buy me
a pink Smith Corona portable typewriter in a pink
case, so I could be the writer she knew I wanted to be.

Moll Flanders, Zia Louisa, and Me

Ah, Moll Flanders. Of all the characters
in those novels I read when I was still
young and in grad school, it's you I remember,
flamboyant, sensual, in love with life.

You always looked for the "Main Chance"
and I, who can barely remember a name
five minutes after I hear it, remember yours.

I knew you were self-serving, but I loved
that you never lied about it,
that you never made excuses,

and I imagine you trying to make your way
in 17th century-England, where a woman on her own
would have been vulnerable, a victim.

You remind me of my Zia Louisa, that woman
who married four times,
who wore
        a tan-colored corset with lace stays
        that had to be pulled tight to hold in
        her large breasts and belly,
who loved to dance the Tarantella,
        her whole body exhilarating
        in moving and stomping.

And though I know Moll only through a book,
I know Zia Louisa from my childhood,
watched her move
like an armored vehicle through life,

past three dead husbands and onto a fourth,
handsome, elegant Zio Guillermo.

They lived in the small apartment above us
on 17th Street in Paterson, NJ.
My mother told me that in the night she'd hear
Zia Louisa crying, but in the morning
she'd come down the back steps,
her cotton dress stiff with starch,
her lace handkerchief tucked in her sleeve,
and she'd be smiling and laughing.

She never told my mother
what sorrow she carried hidden in her sleeve.

The world does not want to know,
and you are mistaken
if you think you heard wild sobbing
in the night.

Ode to My First Car

When I was twenty-one, my father took me to Joe Smith's
Auto Sales on Market Street in Paterson,
to buy a used car. I had just graduated from college
and I was due to start my first real job the next week.
We bought a royal blue VW Bug
with a sunroof and stick shift. I didn't know
how to drive it, so my father drove it home.

My brother-in-law came to my house later in the week
to teach me how to drive. He gave me two lessons
before I had to drive from Hawthorne to Elizabeth
for my job training.

That first day, driving my shiny one-year-old VW,
I discovered that although my brother-in-law taught me
how to drive in a straight line,
he neglected to teach me to downshift,
so on the highway, every time I had to slow down,
I stopped the car and had to start over, moving
into second and third gear. Drivers swerved
around me honking their horns.
I made it through that first week without killing anyone,
and finally my brother-in-law taught me how to downshift.

From then on I'd pick up my friends—Diane, Barbara, Judy—
and we'd be off for rides around Bergen County.
We'd ride around for hours, sometimes, we'd ride
to Greenwood Lake and watch the moon rise over the trees
or we'd go to the Jersey shore, the sunroof open,
the wind in our hair, our hearts full of such exquisite joy,
we thought our bodies couldn't contain it.

Driving late at night, Frank Sinatra and Billy Eckstine
and Johnny Mathis on the radio, a stillness would fall over us,
caught as we were in our separate skins,
our hearts imagining the day we would meet the men
we'd fall in love with for the rest of our lives,
reaching toward the happy ending
we were sure we deserved.

My Father's Red Car

When I think of you, I see you first in your little red car,
the one you bought secondhand, the one mom hated
because she thought it was too flashy and she didn't want to be noticed.
She never climbed in or out of that car
without complaining about the color, but you were happy with it.
You drove it until you were eighty-six
when the police reported to my brother, the doctor,
that you drove the car five miles per hour
and you were going to cause an accident,
so you had to give it up.

Until then, you drove to play cards with your friends in the afternoon
or to visit your sister in Paterson
or to work in the Italian societies
or to do taxes for the other immigrants.
You climbed out of that sporty car
even when you had to use a walker,
nothing stopped you.
I wish I had told you before you died at ninety-two
how much your courage,
your joy in life meant to me,
how much it taught me about how to live.

My nineteen-year-old grandson took me to buy a new car last month.
It's just as flashy and cherry red as the car you drove all those years ago.
I know I'm about twenty-five years too old for the car.
(Did you know that too, about yours?)
But I love tooling around in it.
I love that my grandson chose it for me,
that every time I get into it,
I think of you.

My Father Used to Stay Out Late

when he spent the evening at the Società Cilentana.
He came home whistling.
My mother waited for him in the old brown rocker
while she sewed the sleeves in coats,
basting the sleeves in first and then, in small even stitches,
she'd attach the sleeve to the coat.
He'd come in smelling of wine
and he'd be smiling.
He loved hanging out with his friends,
playing cards and bocce or flirting
with the women from the Ladies' Auxiliary.
My mother stayed home with us.

Even when she was dying at seventy-eight,
she was furious at Anna Bellaqua
who had always had her eye on my father,
still furious that for years,
he went every afternoon to play cards with Anna,
whose husband was twenty years older than she and senile.

When my father couldn't walk anymore, couldn't drive a car,
my mother lifted him from his wheelchair to his chair
where he could watch TV or read the paper,
wrapped the wool blanket around his legs,
put on clean flannel shirts and wool cardigans
and for the first time in more than fifty years together,
my daughter said, "Now she's got him",
in his brown recliner from Medicare,
where he could only dream of his evenings at the Società
and afternoons playing cards with Anna Bellaqua.

Ginestra and Cotton Sheets

My mother, when she was a girl living on that mountain top in Italy,
did not have cotton. They used, instead, a wild plant called *ginestra*
which they dried and wove into fabric for towels and clothes.
It was rough and strong.
My mother embroidered a small red rose
on each towel and then she brought them
with her from Italy in a black metal trunk that became part of her dowry.
She would not enter her marriage without linens to use in her new life.
In America, she got a job sewing the lining in the coats
in a factory filled with other immigrant women
who were also paid by the pieces they finished.
What she wanted for each of her children was to fill a trunk with *biancheria*,
linens we would use in our own married lives,
so she bought white cotton sheets and pillowcases
and put them aside in a trunk to keep them pristine.
My mother loved the cotton sheets she bought for herself
and she wanted us to have them, too. What I remember in my girlhood bed
was slipping between those cotton sheets
that my mother had washed in the wringer washer
and hung out on the line in the backyard to dry in the sun.
The sheets were smooth and beautiful, softened
by my mother's washing,
by hanging them out in the fresh air to dry,
by the iron she used to smooth out any wrinkles.
My bed, with her cotton sheets, smelled of sun and fresh air,
an aroma I remember, even now,
so many years since that time as a young girl
when I'd slide into those cotton sheets
where I always felt safe and loved.

Love Song to HO Cream Farina

When he was thirty-three, my father had surgery to remove a tumor in
    his back.
He was in St. Joseph's Hospital in Paterson for three months.
They told him he was lucky to be alive,
but the surgery left him with a limp he had for the rest of his life.
For a year, he could not work.
My father was a proud man.
He and my mother had saved $300.
They lived on it for a year.
My father would not allow my mother to apply for welfare
which he thought of as a shameful thing to do
so instead we lived on spaghetti and farina
and homemade bread for a year.

My daughter calls me from Boston,
tells me her boyfriend made them all farina
and they loved it, even the kids,
and though I should, I suppose, hate farina
for reminding me how poor we were that year,
instead, even the word comforts me
surrounded as it is in memory
by my mother's love for us.

We didn't know until she was dying,
that all she had was that $300 to last that year
and that's why we ate so much farina.

When I tell my daughter about the $300 and the farina,
her boyfriend says that when they didn't have money,
they waited until his brother came home
from his job at Kentucky Fried Chicken.
He'd bring home the leftovers every night for dinner.

Even now, her boyfriend says that he can't stand the smell of it
and he drives five blocks out of the way
so he doesn't have to smell it or see it.

I can see the kitchen on 17th street,
my mother's hands always busy,
the steaming bowl of farina,
the way it filled us with warmth,
oblivious as we were to the cliff
that waited for us right outside the door.

The Year Our Daughter Was Born

The year our daughter was born
we traded in my blue VW Bug with the sunroof,
that car that glowed like a jewel in the sun,
for a staid brown Plymouth sedan with room enough
for the baby bed and the car seat and all the other paraphernalia two
    children require.
This car could have been our parents' car,
so reliable and lacking in pizzazz it was,
but we drove it to Kansas City
for your first teaching job after you got your doctorate.
We were so young though, we didn't know it then,
driving that old, uncool person's car, our children playing in the back seat.
The other day you unearthed a picture of Jennifer at two with her blonde
    mop of curls.
She is standing in the back yard of the Overland Park, Kansas house
where we lived that first year we were in the Midwest
and she is wearing a pretty pinafore that a friend made for her with a
    matching purse.
That picture hurls me back all the years to those moments
when we held carelessly in our hands
all the things we didn't know we'd lose.

The next year, after we realized that Plymouth was an old fuddy-duddy's car,
we traded it in for a VW bus. It was 1970. We thought we were hippies
because we had friends who were and they lived in a commune.

I went to a consciousness-raising group.
My friend watched my children while I taught.
We bought a house on Oak Street in Kansas City;
the house looked like *Tara* with its high white columns.
I loved the breakfast room and I painted blue chickens
all around the chair rail in the big, old-fashioned kitchen.

49

I volunteered in the Quaker Peace Center,
counseling young men how to apply for conscientious objector status.
I wanted to be cool. We both did, but inside,
that little Italian Catholic girl who obeyed all the rules
still lived and breathed
and would not let me go.

The Houses I Lived In

When we were still young, you and I,
twenty-seven years old and our children, two and four,
we lived in a big white house on Oak Street
in Kansas City, Missouri, a couple of blocks
from the university where we taught,
that stone house, with columns
that stretched from the porch
all the way to the roof,
that house that I loved the moment I saw it,
had bedrooms flooded with light,
each with five big windows,
and an old-fashioned kitchen, where I painted
blue chickens all around the room above the chair rail,
that house, with its separate breakfast room
and it's built-in china closet,
whose glass I stained bright blue and red,
that house, with its extra room
that became my office and my TV room,
that house with its back stairs.
I loved that house because
when I was a child, my family lived
in four small rooms, but I wanted
that "Father Knows Best House,"
the separate bedroom for me,
the book-lined study and curving stairs.
Every time I drove up to the Kansas City house
I would smile, loving the rock-solid look of it,
those huge stone pillars,
and the children in the big playroom,
and the bedroom they chose to share
because, unlike my own dream come true,
their rooms seemed too large to them, too overwhelming,

and Jennifer, at two, with her golden curls,
when she was afraid in the middle of the night,
would crawl into the other bed to be next to her big brother
and John would grumble and complain, but he always let her stay.
I loved that house, but I hated Kansas City.
I was glad to watch it grow smaller
in our rearview mirror when we moved back to New Jersey,
to the house we bought without seeing it,
across the street from my sister's house,
and where I still live now, alone,
no longer young,
where all the rooms, and the loneliness without you, are mine.

The Day the Sky Fell

I used to tell you that you got so sick
because you were always waiting
for the sky to fall and finally it did,
this illness rushing toward us
like the dark funnel cloud
that rushed towards us on those flat Kansas roads
when we were still young
and you said, "Don't worry. It will turn before it gets to us,"
and all I could think of was our two young children
left behind in Kansas City with your parents,
we, miles away in this flimsy VW bus,
my hands white and clutching the door armrest,
and it did turn as you said, but the sky still fell on us,
except it was thirty years later,
and that time we did not escape.

Going Shopping

I used to go shopping with my daughter
when she was a teenager.
I hate stores and hate shopping.
Everything takes time. I get bored.

But I went shopping with my daughter
because she wanted me to go.
I loved watching her try on clothes,
loved seeing how beautiful she looked,
marveled at the perfect bones of her face,
What I did not know about shopping
could have filled the Garden State Plaza Mall,
but I could not deny her anything.
We'd get inside a dressing room
and all my common sense
would fly out the door
and I'd say yes to everything,
as though I could make up
to this child who still lives inside me
for all the clothes I could not afford to buy
when I was young as she is now.
I wanted to give her the life I never had,
an upper-middle-class life tucked into
a silver box with a silver ribbon.

Looking back, I remember how happy I was
to watch her try on the clothes we bought,
how happy that she looked nothing like me.

I had yet to learn
that all of her beauty and grace
would not protect her

from what waited for her
outside the circle
I had drawn around her.

My Hand Remembers

When I speak to my daughter on the phone,
when she calls me on the way to the university,
I ask about the children, ask about Stephen, the house.
I say, "Do you think the upstairs will be finished soon?"
And she tells me that Stephen says it's the closest it's ever been;
and she cracks back that she is as close as she's ever been to death, too.
I love her sense of humor, her quick wit,
the easy way she's taken on cherishing his children,
caring for them as if they were her own.
She tells me she tries to get Indigo to practice her spelling.
Indigo asks her, *Do you want me to be Clara?* (the smartest girl in her class),
I'm not Clara. I am Indigo.
Jennifer says that Indigo needs to learn how to spell.
Jennifer looks over the eight-page essay that the child has written.
Almost every word is misspelled.
Jennifer carefully writes the words out on 3 x 5 cards for her,
and then she teaches her to spell them.
Indigo is going to be a brilliant mathematician or scientist
and words are not magical to her or as sacred as they are to Jennifer.
But Indigo always has an argument ready and never gives up.
Jennifer finds books she loved when she was a girl
and reads them to Indigo just as I had read them to Jennifer.
How grateful I am to have this daughter with her open heart; her stepdaughter
reminds me of Jennifer as a girl.
This child loves art as much as I do.
When I ask what subjects she loves in school,
she asks if she has to choose only one.
"No," I tell her, "you could choose more than one."
Well, I would choose math and science and art.
When I think of my daughter,
I can still feel her hand in mine
as I read to her in the canopy bed I bought for her

which may have been more for the poor child who still resided inside me.
What gratitude I feel towards her
because of this child that she's brought into my life,
so much gratitude for those moments in my memory of
Jennifer with her gorgeous hair freshly washed, smelling of vanilla shampoo,
the two of us, close under the lamplight, while I read to her
and I want those memories to be as vivid for her,
as I hope Indigo will remember Jennifer's voice reading to her,
Jennifer's arms around her shoulders, her hands stroking her hair.

The Summer Porch

When we were young,
our children in grammar school,
my sister and her family lived across the street from us.
We bought our house while we were still in Kansas City.
My sister and my parents had found it for us.
On summer evenings we'd sit on my sister's big front porch,
talking late into the evening,
while the children played in the street,
or sat on the end of the porch playing games while we chatted.
This was before my sister got sick,
before the rheumatoid arthritis
twisted her hands and feet into unrecognizable shapes.
She was still beautiful then with her incredible skin,
her huge brown eyes, her full mouth, her sexy body.

We'd sit and gossip.
The air rustled with the movement of the huge oaks that lined the street.
Strange how we don't recognize those moments
that will glow and sparkle in our memories like fireflies,
don't know how looking back,
those moments are the treasure we will carry
to soothe us against all the losses that lie ahead,
those evenings on the summer porch,

so perfect—all of us still so young and pleased with ourselves
and blind to the blade of the future that hung over our heads.

Ode to Something Once Lost

Something once lost cannot be reclaimed,
the moment slides out of our hands like water
and we can never go back to change what we did
or did not say, we cannot alter the past
to find the words that didn't come to us,
the ones that trembled in our throats.

Once, fifty years ago, a young woman
who claimed to be my friend
mocked me in front of a group of women
and I, who would never usually say anything to defend myself,
turned on her like a wildcat,
told her that she was insulting and rude
to me and everyone else, that the others
were afraid of her and that I never wanted
to go anywhere with her again.

The next day, she shoved an envelope
under my door and when I picked it up
and opened it, there was a Band-Aid on a piece of paper
and she wrote *I apologize.*
Can't we be friends again?
My heart was a stone,
anger like a fire inside me. I called her. We talked.
I wish I could say I forgave her
but there was always a small corner of my heart
that remained closed to her.
Our friendship once shattered could not be repaired
and I'm ashamed to say
even fifty years later,
I still do not forgive her.

The First Dead Person I Saw

The first dead person I saw was Judy's Aunt Louise.
She died, though she was still young and beautiful.
We didn't know what did her in.
We were eight years old and they let us walk past Louise's coffin
set up in the parlor of Judy's grandmother's apartment.
Her aunt said that Louise looked very peaceful and pretty,
but to me, she looked like a wax doll,
and the part of her that made her Louise,
her ready laugh, her smiles, her trips to Europe, all gone.

Years later, in that hospital where I held my mother's hand
when she was dying, she looked right at me, smiled
and then she was gone, just like that.
Her eyes suddenly opaque, everything that made my mother the person
she was, there one minute, gone the next.
The body left on the hospital bed was empty
without her energy, her earthy humor, her ability to soothe and heal.
Even when they laid her out in her coffin
in the beautiful lilac-colored dress I had bought her for my niece's wedding,
even when they put makeup on her face
and folded her hands across her chest,
no matter how much I pretended to myself,
I knew she wasn't there, that she had escaped, at last,
the cancer that destroyed her body.
That moment before she died, the small smile on her face,
the way she looked at me,
a photograph I could clip and shape to fit in a locket
I will carry with me until the day when my own eyes turn to frosted glass.

Badge of Embarrassment

When I was growing up,
I was embarrassed by my Italian parents,
their English stuck on their tongues.
They wore their foreignness like a badge
I knew everyone in the world could see.
Now years after they both have died, I realize
that all the things about them that made
me feel ashamed are the very things
that I now remember:
the old black coal stove with its pots
bubbling on its surface,
my mother's bread baking in the oven,
that table that always had room for one more.
My parents who had nothing but their big hearts,
the circle they drew around us to keep us safe,
and the place they made for others to join us at our table,
the way they taught us by what they did
to love each other and the world.

Cheap

cheap, what I felt about myself when I wore the jeans
that my mother bought for me,
the jeans that were made of black material instead of blue,
cheap jeans she bought on sale
that screamed they weren't the real thing,
cheap, all the times when I said the wrong thing
because I didn't know any better,
cheap, all the things I didn't understand,
how to set a table,
which fork or spoon to use,
how to pick up sugar cubes with silver tongs,
the kind of clothes appropriate to wear
to cocktail parties in Scarsdale, and the tacky way I felt
when I read at Trinity College and the president's wife and the female faculty
all wore pleated skirts and white broadcloth blouses and leather pumps
when I chose to wear a dress with flowers all over it,
cheap, and once again all wrong,
standing out like a cattail among long-stemmed roses,
like the red plastic purse my mother bought me one Christmas,
when I looked at it, I tried to look pleased
but I knew I would never carry that tacky red purse,
loud and ugly, telling everyone where I came from,
where I could never go.

I Carry Shame with Me

How many hours have I spent drowning in shame?
Looking back, I think I lived my whole childhood drenched
in it—ashamed of my father's job, my own dark skin,
my cheap clothes, so many ways I found to hate myself,
ashamed of the life I was born to, the raggedy street,
though my mother swept the sidewalk and stoop every day,
though our flat was scrubbed to a shine,
nothing could change the light bulb on a cord that dangled
over the table, the oilcloth smell permeating the kitchen,
the girls in seventh grade who came to our house for lunch
and laughed behind their hands
at my mother's broken English.

Shame was the dress I wore
and the one I wear all these years later,
when the little girl in her hand-me-down clothes appears
and I say something as I did the other day
to a tall, slender woman. "Oh, I want your body—"
and as soon as I say it, I realize how strange I sound.
I try to explain that I meant to say
I want to be tall and slim like you, and instead
it came out like a proposition.

"That was the nicest thing anyone has said to me in years,
and now you want to take it back," she replies,
my face stained with shame, like that terrified girl
I thought I'd left behind years ago
on the cracked sidewalks of Paterson.

I Always Wanted to Come From

I always want to come from a town
with wide, tree-lined streets,
with big white colonial houses,
a town like Ridgewood or Glen Rock,
a town with families with a father who commuted
to work in New York City on the train,
who wore a three-piece suit and silk tie,
and carried a briefcase,
while the mother took care of their house all day,
making it ready for the father to come home.

I didn't want to come from a town
where houses were split up into apartments,
where alleyways ran along one side of the buildings,
alleyways that led to the back stoop and back door
that all visitors used. I didn't want to come from a town
where no one ever used the front door,
with a mother and father who worked in factories,
where there was never enough money for even the smallest luxury,
where people spoke broken English
and believed that girls should get married at eighteen.

Looking back at all the things I hated
and the things that I longed for,
I have since gotten—
the one-family house with the curving stairs,
the huge living room and dining room,
the American life I yearned for.
But when I hold all those things that I finally achieved in my hand, I realize
that I forgot to be grateful for everything I had before—
the big table full of my mother's food,
the laughter and talk and closeness,

the things my parents taught me by the way that they lived—
how to open up my arms to the world,
how to welcome others in,
that I might never have learned
if I had lived in a Ridgewood colonial
with parents who did not understand the secret of joy.

Claiming My True Name

It took me years to claim my true name,
so many years layered in shame,
so many years trying to hide my immigrant self and my true name.
Looking back, I know what I wanted when I saw you,
Love, that first time at your friend's house,
you with your blond boyish looks, your handsome face,
your wide gray eyes,
your big white colonial house,
your educated American parents.
Did I imagine that by marrying you
I could erase all those z's and t's in my name,
change it all like an old coat I could give away,
and put on instead what I thought
was the sleek Americanness of your name
and I would be able to erase my ethnic face,
my frizzy hair?
How I wanted to deny the foreign girl I was,
the one who didn't speak English when I went to school,
deny my Italian parents and the cold-water flat,
leave them all behind and slide
right into the life of America that I was sure I wanted.
Years later, I realized I had traded away everything
that shaped me, traded away

this song that beat in my blood,
the aroma of the ethnic food I loved,
and only then staring into a void as big as the Grand Canyon,
did I claim my true name,
wrap all those z's and t's around me
and force people to use my true name,
even when they stumble over it and they have to ask,
"Is this the way you pronounce your name?"

And I pronounce it for them,
waving it in the air like a banner,
proud of my Italian-self,
proud of all the things that marked me
as unique, as different, a foreign creature
who can at last claim my own true name.

What My Father Taught Me

Why is it only now
so many years after you died that I realize
how much you taught me by the way you lived your life,
how you reached out to others,
how you always offered to help,
how you always let cars go ahead of you
when you were waiting to turn onto a busy road.

How many times did I mock you?
How impatient and rude I was,
annoyed by your wide smile,
your crooked teeth,
the way you drank your coffee from a saucer
as all the immigrant Italians did,
that powerless leg you dragged wherever you went.

Now, with my own legs failing me,
I can see you struggling to keep on doing everything you could.
Outgoing, joyous, fun-loving, you were secretary of the Società Cilento
in Paterson, NJ for fifty-two years,
kept their books, minutes of each meeting.
So often you drove people to the Italian consulate
to sign papers to bring their families to America.
Every day you visited your friends for a few hours,
cards and conversation until age eight-six,
when you could no longer drive.
Even when you were in a wheelchair,
nothing could still your curious mind,
your love of politics and history,
your mathematical intelligence.

We were so alike you and I,
both loving people,
loving being there for others and hearing their stories,
both ready to reach out to the world and to others.
I wish I could tell you what I should have told you
when you were still alive,
how much you taught me about courage and never giving up.
Forgive me for all I didn't understand,
for wanting you to be the middle-class father you could never be.

Praise to you for all you taught me about generosity and grace,
for never forgetting how to laugh,
and for always opening your arms and welcoming others in.

Mistakes I Have Made

All of my mistakes live inside me,
even after seventy years,
their weight, heavy as granite slabs on my back.

The mistake of correcting my mother
when we passed a packaged-goods store—
and she said we should go there someday
to buy fabric because the cloth delivered
to the factory where she worked was labeled packaged goods,
and I laughed at her.
"No, Ma," I said, "that's a liquor store,"
and then I saw her face,
red with humiliation and shame
and no way to pull my own laughter back out of the air.

The mistake I made in wanting my children to have
all the things I did not have—
so I almost drowned them in toys
and I wanted them to go to all the parties and sleepovers.
But this one day, my daughter's friend called and asked her to sleepover
and I said *yes* while my daughter shook her head mouthing to say *no*.
And finally, I understood that I wanted her to do
all the things I had not been allowed to do.
My mistake was that she did not want what I had wanted as a girl.

Mistakes I've made, not understanding that Jimmy,
who was my boyfriend, was gay,
even after he had asked me to go to a gay club with him.
Mistakes. How easy it is to misunderstand.
How hard it is to take back words spoken in anger.

In Georgia, a Lake

In Georgia, a lake almost as large
as the sea, is drying up.
It feels like that this morning
when I meant to say IED
and instead say IUD in a class,
and after I say it, I realize there is
something wrong, but I can't quite
come up with what the acronym is.
Why do acronyms remind me of Geometry,
which I could never master either?

On TV later this morning, I watch
as a broadcaster talks about the closing
of ski resorts in the Sierra Nevada Mountains,
because the drought has destroyed
the snowcaps. "We did everything we could,"
the ski lodge owner tells the camera.
"We moved snow around, but in the end,
we had to close early."

My son insists global warming is a liberal fantasy.
"Weather is cyclical," he tells me.
I wonder why I worked so hard to pay
for all those expensive schools he attended,
if he can be influenced by FOX News.

There's a lake inside me
where my love for my son is,
though it is not enough to close
the distance between us.

Last May in San Mauro, Cilento, 2017

Last May in San Mauro,
my eyes drank in the vistas,
mountains and sea,
the sky a huge bowl above us,
the narrow streets of the town,
cobble-stoned and ancient,
the church at the top of the hill,
the children who sang songs and played music
in my honor and who wanted to take their pictures with me,
and the ladies of the town who made pastries
that I remembered my mother making
in my childhood. How grateful I am
to be surrounded by these generous, cheerful people,
the way they know how to celebrate.

And looking back, I remember them and smile too.
I met several first cousins I had not met before.
I saw again, Maria and Giannina and their husbands.
I felt I had known them all my life
and Professoro Marracco and Maria Giovanna Barra
who had arranged everything for me—
the ceremony and the translation of my poems
and the book they produced with my poems in Italian and English.
How blessed I felt to be in this place where my mother was born.
My father grew up in Galdo, the town above San Mauro.
It must have been so hard to leave a place so exquisitely beautiful,
it's air and water, clear and clean,
to leave their families behind, knowing they would not see them again.

This fall and summer and winter, when I am beset by illness and accidents,
I take out my memories of San Mauro to hold in my hand

like a favorite jewel, see how it reflects the light, see how beautiful it is. I hold the memories close to give me comfort when I am most afraid.

My Son the Lawyer Quotes Dylan Thomas to Give Me Courage

After I lose my balance and fall,
smashing my nose against the hardwood floor,
I slip in a huge puddle of blood,
try to stand up but my feet keep sliding.

I have always loved mystery stories,
read about people stabbed to death,
but never thought about the blood,
how the murderer could break his neck sliding in it.

After the hospital,
after the x-rays,
the EKG,
the four-hour drive to Binghamton,
after I teach my class, looking battle-scarred,
I think of my son who used to tell me
I should cut back and give up poetry,
proving that he did not understand anything about me.

When I talk to him on the phone he is shocked
to hear defeat in my voice.
I am always optimistic about everything
even in the middle of calamity,
but today I am brought low
by the recognition of frailty.
My son, the lawyer, the practical pragmatic one,
says, *How many women your age have a life they love,*
work they love doing?

Later, he sends me a quote from Dylan Thomas.
"Do not go gentle into that good night,

Old age should burn and rave at close of day;
Rage, rage against the dying of the light."

I repeat the lines over and over to myself,
grateful to this son I was sure didn't understand anything about me.

The Beds I Slept In

The cheap metal three-quarter bed I shared with my sister
when we were growing up was ugly and utilitarian,
but I loved my sister, who let me curl up next to her because I was always cold.

The bed my mother bought when we moved to Hawthorne, that blue-collar
    suburb
not five minutes from the Riverside section of Paterson where I grew up,
was maple with a matching dresser. I shared that bed too, with my sister.

The bed I shared with you when we got married,
a colonial bed from Maiella's furniture store, that bed
where we made love and where we learned to make each other moan.
We left that bed in Kansas City.

Your mother gave us a four-poster bed, mahogany and lovely.
So many years I slept in your arms, traced the beautiful angles of your body,
the high cheekbones of your face; thirty-eight years that bed held us before
    you got sick.
After you died, I slept alone in that mahogany four-poster,
your shadow always there with me.

When I fell and broke my nose in the upstairs hallway,
I moved a twin bed to a corner in our family room
so I wouldn't have to climb the stairs. This twin bed feels
insubstantial after the solid mahogany one we shared for so long,
but I sleep alone there too, and my dreams sometimes
let me watch your face as you sleep.

Contemplating the Moon in My 77th Year

As a girl, I was fascinated by the moon,
thought it was amazing in the dark Paterson sky.
I wrote hundreds of haiku about it.
I always saw it as some reflection of my longing
to live in a place far removed from my ordinary life.

In 1969, in married student housing at Rutgers,
I watched with my two young children,
as Neil Armstrong on the Apollo 11 mission
walked on the moon. It seemed
unbelievable that these figures could be walking
on that cratered surface.

Today, more than fifty years later, I read
that the moon is drifting away from the earth.
Did you know that the dark side of the moon is a myth?

Now, the moon has become a symbol for what is left
of my life, all those craters that trip us up so often,
so we're unable to walk without falling,
like the other day, when I waited for almost an hour
for someone to pick me up off the porch where I had fallen.

I must accept that the landscape of old age
is like the surface of the moon.
As a girl, I made up stories about its cratered surface,
the faces I imagined lived in it.
I watched those astronauts on the moon, weightless in their space suits.
What did I know? I thought life would be easy
and I would walk across it sure and strong;
instead now this shuffling gait.
I'd like to be weightless

like the men in their spacesuits.
No more broken bones.
No more pitfalls. No more grief.

Moon, each day, you wear a different face.
I still imagine you speak to me.
And you do, but the words I hear
cannot save me; it is your beauty,
as you skim across the night sky,
that lifts me up.

The Day after the Election

On the day after the election,
I wake up to news I hope has to be wrong.
It isn't.
When I began to suspect
that Hillary Clinton would lose, I went to bed
thinking that if I went to sleep, it couldn't happen,
but of course, it did.

I think of my father,
my radical, political father,
in love with the news and newspapers.
I remember the way in 1994 when he could no longer walk,
he wanted me to take him to Washington
to march. "The American people are asleep," he said.

He'd tell me about Mussolini,
how the people fell in love with him,
how he promised that he would save them from poverty and despair.
They believed him until the Brownshirts descended on the town.
And quickly and quietly, anyone who spoke up was put in jail.
That was the end of their new dream,
the beginning of their new reality.

This morning, after the election, I think of my father.
I know he would've wanted to do something,
to stop what was happening to the America he so loved,
this Italian immigrant whose heroes were Roosevelt and JFK,
who believed America was the greatest country in the world.

Each day that passes,
each new cabinet appointment,
people in charge of departments and responsible

for programs they will most likely destroy,
I become more and more discouraged, frightened.

My student says it was no choice between the two candidates
and that's why she didn't vote.
This student has no husband,
has two children,
lives on food stamps and welfare.
She writes about what it is like to be hungry.
She actually believes there was no difference between the two candidates.

I'd like to be strong enough to stop what is happening.
I'd like to have my father's courage.
How can we lose all that he believed, his beautiful America?

I hope my father is peacefully playing cards with his friends
in that heavenly grape arbor, half glasses of wine before them,
peach slices, gleaming like amber in the wine.

Today in the Workshop in Calabria, 2019

Today in the workshop in Calabria, I remembered
our first trip to Italy together.
Because we had been busy
raising our children, this trip
was the first one we had taken without them. Your mother
came to our house to stay with the children
so we could spend two weeks on this tour
traveling to the country of my parents' birth.
We were both bookish people,
unaccustomed to traveling in a group,
but here we were, both of us excited
by this new adventure.

There is a picture; I am seated at a table with others.
You are standing behind me, leaning over to whisper something to me.
I don't remember what you were saying,
but I know that the other people on this trip were years older than we
and they said, "Look at the lovebirds."
Perhaps their words were ironic, perhaps kind.

We hadn't paid much attention to them, although they had seemed
    strange to us,
not because they were so much older
but because they didn't seem excited to see Bernini's horses
and Michelangelo's David or the Sistine Chapel.
They returned to the bus after each stop with their purchases—
watches and rings and cameos,
expensive baubles they could show off when they got home,
while you and I bought nothing and brought instead
the image of this incredible sunlit place,

the art that amazed us
because it was so much more than the images
we had seen in books.

When you died, our daughter made up a board of photographs:
Your parents, mine, you and I together,
but when I looked at the picture of us on that long-ago day,
I asked our daughter, "Who is that woman with Daddy?"
And she said, *What do you mean? That's you.*
I argued, "No, it isn't because the woman in the picture is beautiful, her eyes
huge and alive in her glowing face," and for me,
Beauty was blonde and blue-eyed and placid as a plate,
not a dark-haired girl who seemed to be shooting off sparks of light.
Only now, looking back over the vista of years, do I recognize
all the things about myself I did not know enough to treasure
until time robbed me of all the fire that had lit up my life,
those spectacular moments so long since vanished.

All Those Trips I Took When I Was Still Young

All those trips I took when I was still young—
my first trip to Italy with Dennis.
We booked a tour because we had never been out of the country.

That trip where the bus was full of people
who wanted to shop and show off their purchases,
when all we wanted to do
was see the art we'd only read about before.

All those trips we took: Sicily, Italy, Portugal, Spain, Hawaii,
when Dennis was still strong enough to travel,
we traipsed through museums and down cobbled streets
without ever thanking our bodies.

Then the trip to read poetry with Laura
when we traveled together for ten days of poetry in Sicily.
We read our poems in English.
Our translators read in Italian.

All those trips over the next thirty years
to Yugoslavia, Wales, St. Petersburg, Finland, Malta,
and my many trips to Italy and Sicily
to read at universities and cultural centers.

Time passes so quickly.
We thought we would always be strong enough for these journeys,
and now my trips are limited
to three turns around the house with my walker,
hours in my Barcalounger, where I fall asleep,
too tired to even dream about the places I will go.
I, with my optimist's heart, no longer believe
that I am strong enough to take any more trips.

I think of my neighbor,
who at eighty-seven, took a European cruise
despite her son's objections.
I remember her telling me,
"I don't have to get off the ship if I'm too tired."
That's the same spirit I always thought that I had,
though it seems to have vanished
and I feel fragile and as transparent
as a dragonfly's wings.

In the Photograph, I Am Sixteen

—Written in IDS poetry workshop, Il Nibbio, Morano, Calabria, 2019

In the photograph, I am sixteen
and dressed for a high school prom.
My dress is light blue, a color I chose
because I wanted to be blonde and not me
with my olive-tone skin and dark frizzy hair. I am thin and high-breasted.
The dress is fitted carefully over my body and slender waist
and then swirls out to a bottom that is lifted by two crinolines.
It's the 1950s. These are the kinds of clothes all the girls are wearing.
I have on high heels and nylons held up by a garter belt.

I was shy and uncomfortable. I barely spoke outside the house
although at home, with my Italian family, I was exuberant,
words tumbling out over themselves as I spoke.
It was only in poetry that I found a way
to live in America,
in poetry that I could express all the dreams
that filled me with longing.
In my poems, I could be the strong independent person
I imagined myself to be at some future time.

I am sixteen, my life ahead of me,
the long road I have yet to climb
is just as shrouded in mystery as these Calabrian mountains
where I sit writing this poem today.
So many years have passed since that photograph
in the dress that was pale blue,
and it took me years
to realize it was covering the bright red spirit inside me.

What Do I Know about Grief
—For Maria Lisella

What do I know about grief
or how Death would follow me like a determined lover,
taking first my mother, father, sister, my best friend of forty-two years,
then my husband, more friends each year,
how his bony finger would point at the next person.
Once I walked into a spider web and I think grief is like that—
it catches in your hair and your lashes.

My friend's husband died after a short and brutal illness.
They were close as two spoons. When he died,
she told me she had always been happy
just to be in their apartment with him,
even passing him in the hallway felt like an act of love.

In the weeks after my husband died,
in the months waterlogged with tears,
I thought I would not survive, but gradually
I began to imagine that he came back to visit me,
a shadow in the corner of the room,
a presence sitting in a chair beside me,
though, of course, he could never stay long.
I am comforted by his ghost self.
I am sure he is telling me that he is content in that other world
where I cannot touch him.
I am grateful there is a door
through which he can pass to visit me,
even for a moment, his ghost hand on my cheek.

Ghost Voices

Ghost voices surround me like fog,
all my dead still live inside me
even years after they have passed
over to that other world.
My mother's voice, sardonic and practical,
my mother, who spent a lot of time criticizing everything I did,
although she said if she didn't tell me, who would?
My mother, who held me at her round kitchen table,
patting my back, saying, *Cry, cry. It will do you good,*
though she told me she had forgotten how to cry.
My father's voice telling stories of his younger days
after he arrived from Italy at sixteen,
stories of how he met my mother,
stories of the heroes he'd so admired—
JFK and FDR, my political, radical father
sitting with me every night after my mother died.

My sister, her voice wobbly, calling me at 7 p.m.
asking when I was going to be at her house,
my sister, who was ill and frightened, so much so,
she also needed me to just sit and hold her fragile hand
while she talked about her life and all she remembered.

My husband, so athletic and strong, beset by illness
that robbed him of everything he cherished—
swimming, running, riding his bike, driving a car,
even his mind,
and his voice, softer and softer, almost a whisper,
his voice saying *I love you* into my ear,
his world populated by ghosts
who came to visit him in the months before he died,
ghosts, who told him they were saving a place for him.

The others that I have lost,
now wait their turn to speak,
but my ancestors' voices
I can only imagine since I never met them,
left behind in Italy,
where the only words they had for me
were in letters that made my mother's heart ache.
They too, have become ghosts.
Is that the fate of all of us?

All we can hope is that our own voices
will remain inside those who loved us,
to be comforted for as long as they need to hear us.

My Mother's Greatest Fear

My mother left Italy when she was twenty-three.
She left her mother behind in San Mauro,
that medieval village on the top of a mountain.
She never saw her mother again.
She'd only known my father three months
before she married him.
My mother and her new husband
were supposed to board the ship together
to sail to New York, but the official
turned her away at the berth.
Her papers were not in order
so my father had to leave without her.

The rules of "the old way"
meant that she could not go back
to live with her own mother.
My mother, who had only left San Mauro
once in her life to go to Rome on her honeymoon,
had no choice but to stay in her husband's village,
to live with her new mother-in-law—it was the old way.
Her mother-in-law cooked *pasta e fagioli*
every day, and every day my mother threw up.
Her mother-in-law did not want
my mother's help with the cooking,
my mother who was a brilliant cook,
who had been cooking good meals
every night for her family
since she was nine years old.
Those six months that she spent there
seemed interminable.

When she finally arrived in New York Harbor,
she was six months pregnant.
She survived the journey in steerage,
seasick and weak.
She saw my father on the dock.
She knew how fortunate
she was to have married a man
who had come back to Italy
to find a wife, how lucky,
that she loved him and he loved her.

My mother knew from the other women
who sewed beside her in the factories of Paterson,
how many were not as fortunate,
how many had also married men they barely knew
because that was the old way,
only to be beaten each day,
to be slapped with words so caustic,
they left scars.

My mother's greatest fear was that we
would end up somewhere
far away from her, as she had done
with her own mother, that we would have no one to turn to
in times of trouble.
She wanted the family to be together,
to always be there for one another
so that even after she was gone
and couldn't protect us,
we would have each other.

My older sister took me with her
when she went out with her friends.
I took my brother to the barbershop

or the candy store.
In the years when my sister was dying,
I crossed the street from my house to hers.
I held her fragile hand in mine and we
talked and talked. To this day,
my younger brother, the doctor, always treats me
as though I am his most important patient.
All my beloved dead,
my mother, father, sister
and husband live in memory,
a light that burns no matter
how many years go by

and I say to my dead mother,
"Don't be afraid, Ma, we
are still together,
the living and the dead
and nothing to fear, we
still have each other
just as you wanted."

Chalk Dust and Light

In the ballroom at the Marriott in Albany, NY,
in the middle of this conference, I remember
suddenly Miss Ferraro's voice in fifth grade
when she read poems and stories to us,
her big eyes soft as a doe's, her generous mouth,
her love of words
and how her love of those words
made us love them, too.
Miss Ferraro, I write to you today from a distance
of sixty-four years, to thank you for all those hours
of reading aloud in the dusty classroom of PS 18,
for treating me as if I were your child,
for touching my arm when you passed me in the aisle,
for filling that classroom with chalk dust and light,
the light that came from you,
the husky voice I still remember.
Thank you for the way you changed my life,
opened doors inside me I didn't know were there,
for teaching me that books could take me away
to places I'd never been, to places I might never see.

Meatloaf and Hamburger Helper

Growing up, my mother cooked
macaroni and gravy, meatballs
and *braciola*, spinach, lentil soup,
and roasted chicken and potatoes,
made *zeppole*, big salads fresh from the garden,
zucchini with rosemary,
meals so delicious I can still taste them.
When my children were growing up,
my mother-in-law taught me
to make American food that
my husband liked because
he grew up on it—so I learned
how to make pot roast, and leg of lamb,
and stew, and roast beef,
pork chops, and steak, and baked potatoes.
She taught me how to make meatloaf
which was cheap and could be used
for one meal plus sandwiches.
She taught me to make meals with Hamburger Helper
which my mother called junk. Years later, my stomach
turns at the thought of Hamburger Helper,
the greasy feel of it, the fake
chemical taste of sauce and spices,
flavor created in a lab,
but when I served those meals,
so different from anything my mother
ever cooked, I felt I had arrived
in middle-class America, that I now belonged
in the land that almost guaranteed you'd die
of a heart attack before you could reach old age
and not the land of my father,
too poor to buy all this meat

even if he had wanted it, my father
who died at ninety-two, sitting in the sun in his garden,
the aroma of tomatoes and peppers and zucchini
perfuming the air around him.

Snow Falls Thick

outside the windows of Saint Marguerite retreat house.
If only my mother had not died more than twenty years ago, I'd call her,
tell her, my practical, no-nonsense mother, to stop working
long enough to look out into the softening December world,
here in this peaceful place where no sound enters.

Memory pulls me back
to the 17th Street kitchen with its coal stove
and sweet, bread-baking aroma.
It is 1947. We are having a huge blizzard
and all the windows in our apartment frost over in patterns
that seem to me to be exquisitely beautiful.
My mother gives me a potato fresh from the oven.
I hold the hot potato, its crunchy skin, in my hand,
and I realize how much more my mother offered
when she gave me that warmth to hold in my hands.

Apparitions

How many ghosts can gather in one house?
If you had asked me twenty-five years ago,
I would not have known how to answer,
but now too many years crammed with loss,
too many of the people I love, gone,
to that other country where I cannot touch them.
But some days I swear all of them gather,
one by one, at my table as they did
all those years ago on holidays.
I am glad to see them
though they speak a language I no longer understand.
I want to know about the country they now call home.
I put out small cups of espresso and pastries and anisette.
I know they're happy to see me,
to fill my house again with their presence
and their chirpy voices and their laughter.
I wish they still spoke my language,
but I too, am happy to be with them—
my husband, my mother, father, sister,
cousin, aunts, uncles, best friends for years.
Their ghost arms encircle me.
I beg them to stay longer but I understand
they need to go back.
Their bodies gradually vanish
as though they are made of smoke
and they rise up and drift off
though I call and call their names.

I Can Still See My Mother

in her cotton house dress stiff with starch,
her neat self in sensible shoes,
her hair combed and home-styled,
nothing fancy or elegant about her.
She was a woman that we knew
we could lean on
and we did.

I had migraine headaches
when I was growing up
and my mother would say— first let's see
if you have *malocchio*, The Evil Eye.

And she would take out a bowl
and fill it with water
and set a jar of olive oil on the table
along with a big black-handled knife.
Then she would put some drops of oil in the water
and she would whisper a prayer
and watch to see
if oil drops would open up and spread
and if they did, she'd say, *you have malocchio*.
She'd take the knife and mutter an incantation,
and then she'd slice across the bowl and wave the knife in the air three times.
Then she would fake spit into the air and touch the tip of the knife
to my forehead and add one more prayer.
After, she'd say, "That was bad, but now it's gone."
Each time, she worked her magic. The headache disappeared.

When I lived in Kansas City,
I'd call her on the phone and ask for the ritual
and my headache would vanish.

We all believed she had this power to heal,
even my sister, the nurse, who would murder me for telling
that when she was a girl, she too, went to our mother for this cure.
And now, twenty years after my mother's death,
my sister calls and asks if I know how to do *malocchio*.
I say, "Yes. Dad wrote it down for me."
And I imitate my mother,
hoping I sound like her, so she believes I have my mother's power
though I don't believe it myself.
I try to channel her,
mumbling and spitting and waving the black-handled knife
over the bowl, like she did when I was young
and I still believed my mother could do anything.
I was sure she could break the spell of evil that someone had cast upon me.

So many days now I wish I still believed
a bowl of water, olive oil, a black-handled knife
and mumbled prayer could save me.

In the Photo of Us

In San Mauro, I gather with my cousins whom I never met before.
They are the children of my grandfather's brother.
One of them tells me she has a photo she wants to show me,
and she hands me the picture. On the back is a note
my father had written to his mother, dated 1945,
so he would have been thirty-nine,
younger than my own children are now.

In that photo, I am about five years old, skinny
and big-eyed and wearing a dress
that has embroidery on the front and little puff sleeves.
It is an expensive-looking dress,
so I know it must have been a hand-me-down from
Zia Christina's late-in-life daughter.
Next to me, my two-year-old
brother is seated in a chair. His face is sweet and open.
He is wearing dress pants,
brown leather shoes and white socks.
His hair is in a bowl cut.
On the other side of him, my sister stands.
Her dress looks like a hand-me-down too,
but she would have been the wrong size
to be given the same clothes I was given,
so the dress looks raggedy and worn.

When I send the picture to my brother,
he says, *We could have been people
from the Dust Bowl, we look so poor.*

"But Al", I say, "we were so lucky!
We had Mom and Dad and each other.

When you look at us, who would have thought
that these three children would end up a writer, a doctor, and a nurse?"

He agrees, but still, I can tell he is shocked
to understand just how the world would have seen us,
what they expected us to do,
and how we proved them wrong.

In the Shimmering Dusk

17th Street turns silver as it darkens
and evening lays its grey blanket
over the quiet street
and vacant lots
and immigrant gardens,
though the Paterson of my childhood
no longer exists,
the Paterson of memory
is bright as burning coal,
like the coal my mother
shoveled in the stove
that heated the 17th Street
kitchen when I was a child.

How fortunate we were
to hold so much light in
our hands like the lightning bugs
we caught in mason jars
that lit up the night-dark stoop,
their lamps flashing on and off.
We'd sit in a circle on the stoop—
Big Joey, Little Joey, Ralphie
and Laura and Alex,
and tell stories to scare each other
especially Alex, the youngest of us,
whose eyes were wide and round as silver dollars.
Then our mothers would call us home.
Alex, Laura and I would
enter our lit kitchen and my mother
would give us hot milk with Bosco in it
and graham crackers.

And we'd put on our cotton pajamas,
climb into our beds and go to sleep.

My own children played on Oak Place
in the summer evenings
while we sat on my sister's front porch
and watched, the street
always full of noise and laughter.

My grandchildren in their big houses,
in their expensive neighborhoods,
live on streets that are empty of life.

Children go on play dates
that are arranged by their parents
or take lessons in Russian, math or violin.
But the freedom I remember
looking back at my own childhood
is absent. I am sad that these children
will not have such warm memories
to carry them into their own old age.

What Does the Child Inside Me Still Want

—Written in IDS poetry workshop, Il Nibbio, Morano, Calabria, 2019

How many years have I spent
trying to appease the child who still
cowers inside me—that being
who did not know how to find the words to free it
from the prison of her circumstances,
poverty knotted around her throat,
the dreams of another life that seemed beyond reach
for this child of immigrants
who did not speak English when she went to school,
that child who found in poetry,
a way to articulate all she longed for,
how to fill in the outline of herself;
she never could've explained it out loud to anyone else.
Even today, so many years after those first poems,
my books piled around me,
there are days within the darkest corners of myself,
that child still cries though she cannot say why
or what she wants,
that high-pitched wail of hunger
whose exact nature she cannot name.
Is that why so many things
I worked so hard to give my children—the private schools
and slumber parties and summer camps and good clothes—
are really for the child
with her hand-me-down clothes and her cotton underpants for Christmas
    presents,
for all the toys she never got
because she didn't know how to ask
for what she needed and could not name?

Even After All These Years

Even after all these years,
a plate of spaghetti gives me
comfort, the food my mother made
three times a week
when I was a child in the 17th Street tenement,
that food we ate every day
the year my father was too sick to work,
so we had spaghetti and HO Cream Farina,
that food that still fills some hollow place inside me.

Our mother made loaves of homemade bread,
stirred the tomato sauce that we called gravy
that was nothing like my mother-in-law's gravy,
which was brown, that was made from cooking roasts.
We didn't have meat. We couldn't afford it
except for meatballs and *braciola*.

I suppose I should remember with bitterness
how poor we were, but what I remember
is our mother working at the coal stove
her body turning toward us,
her quick hands scooping spaghetti onto to our plates,
steam rising from the homemade gravy.
She'd add a sprinkle of Parmesan cheese
sent fresh in a block from Italy
that she grated to a fine powder on the tin grater.

Even today, when I am sad or lonely,
a plate of spaghetti makes me feel
my mother's presence, soothing
and beckoning me home.

Approaching Morano

The road is all curves and sharp bends,
and with each turn,
more of Morano comes into view.
First I see the mountains, steeped in mist.
As we drive closer, the houses
built into the sides of the mountains emerge,
and fields of wildflowers that grow along the road,
and then at last, the Albergo San Domenico,
with its intricate wrought iron gate and pergola
and huge rose bushes that are in full bloom
though it's so cold out that the school children,
led by their teachers down the side of the road,
are bundled in fluffy winter jackets
and wearing blue and red caps.
Then I see the Albergo itself, elegant in its proportions,
and the proprietors, warm and welcoming.
Our room is like something from the 19th century
and the view from the windows so stunning
in its ancient beauty.

I am sure this landscape has to be some kind of heaven.
The camera in my mind snaps pictures,
clicking, clicking like high-tech equipment,
each shot emblazoned in my memory so that I know,
years from now, I will remember and be comforted.
When I was growing up in that Paterson tenement
separated from the other tenements
that almost leaned on each other like crooked teeth,
I thought I'd never escape.
I could not have imagined even in my brightest dreams,
how far I would travel. As a child, I never left Paterson.
Nothing I knew would have led me to believe

I could leave that narrow world behind,
but today I celebrate the landscape I have come to love,
the way now, at last, I understand how even if my body betrays me
my fierce and hungry spirit drinks in this beauty,
stores these images up to give me courage
for whatever waits for me
at home on the other side of the Atlantic.

Driving Through the Calabrian Landscape

The mountains rise up
in huge humps against the sky.
They circle the horizon.
They almost seem to be stacked up behind each other.
Their color is dark and brooding.
They have been here from the beginning of time
and I think of the people who have been bred here.
How could they be anything but courageous in such a place?

I fall asleep and when I wake up,
the landscape has altered
and we are facing the Tyrrhenian Sea,
the water, aquamarine, and turquoise
against the rocky shore.
Built into the hills, houses are painted white and pastels.
On the beach, chairs are stacked waiting for summer,
the umbrellas not yet unfurled,
the beach deserted except for one family,
a man, sitting at a table looking down,
his wife holding a child in her arms,
while the other child, a boy, plays in the garish plastic playhouse
or jumps on the trampoline.
Watching them, I wonder if they are aware
how separate they seem, or how lucky they are
to be here at the edge of this mystic sea.

Driving back toward Morano, we move once again
toward the humped mountains,
the sky above them packed full of threatening clouds in shades of gray.
In this unfamiliar landscape, I am grateful
for this stark beauty,
for this opportunity to visit a place so otherworldly.

I imagine it is a place of magic and monsters.
Surely, no ordinary people could have survived here.

This Morning on the Terrace

This morning on the terrace at Albidona,
the mourning dove greets me with his repetitive cry.
I look out over the olive trees, planted in neat rows,
leading down to the Ionian Sea, spread out before me
like an abstract painting. It is amazing in its changing colors,
turquoise, green, deep blue, lavender.
The Calabrians tell me the colors change because of the currents
and although I have been to museums all over the world,
I have never seen anything quite like this.
It could be a sea of silk like those scarves artists create.
The sweet-smelling air, the gentle breeze that lifts my hair,
the stillness broken only by the cries of birds.

Celebration in Albidona

Last night we drove to Albidona
where the mayor greeted me
and walked with me to the town library.
She is the first female mayor of the town
which is at least five centuries old.
They have planned a ceremony of welcome,
but when I'm confronted by the stairs
to the library, I say that I'll stay in my wheelchair
and wait for them to come back.
I know I have disappointed them,
but since I can't really walk at the moment,
I don't see how I'm going to climb those stairs,
though I'd like to please them.
Instead, I wait for them in the lane and the mayor
presents me with a plaque and I feel tears
press against the back of my eyes.
I am catapulted back to my childhood,
to ceremonies at the Società Cilento,
all the people who were part of my life
when I was growing up.

Now the mayor walks next to me
while Marco Gatto pushes my chair
to the town square where an old man
plays on the bottle, using a big iron key,
keeping time to the sound of the tambourine and the bagpipe
made from a goat skin. Nearby,
someone plays an accordion,
beautifully crafted from leather
and mother of pearl.
In itself, it is a work of art.
The Albidonesi people tell me that Albidona means golden sunrise.

For me, in this moment,
the town fulfills the promise of its name.
The women of the town have made platters of food—
zeppole made into circles like elongated donuts,
though they have another name for them,
the platter of another delicacy
that are exactly like my mother used to make,
except that she put honey and sprinkles on them.
Then they cart out platters of *capicola* and salami and olives.
Marco's mother apologizes for smelling like oil
because she's been frying all day. I'd bend and kiss her hand
if I weren't afraid she'd think I was insane.
She reminds me of my mother,
as though she has brought her back to me
and I think about her.
I love every minute in this town with its costumed dancers
and its little band and its generosity and hospitality.
I realize how much of Italy my mother had brought with her to Paterson,
how familiar the Calabrian town is,
and though I have never seen them before,
these people are my people.

Acknowledgments

Grateful acknowledgments to the editors of the follwing journals in which these poems, sometimes in early versions, first appeared or are forthcoming: "17th Street, Paterson, NJ, *VIA*, 2016; "In Georgia, a Lake," and "In Our House Nobody Ever Said," *Beyond Baroque*, 2016; "Moll Flanders, Zia Louisa and Me," *Nasty Women's Poets: An Anthology of Subversion Verse*, 2017; "Going Shopping," *Lips*, 2017; "What My Father Taught Me," *Italian Americana*, 2017; "My Mother's Greatest Fear," *San Diego Poetry Annual*, 2017; "Lace Curtains" and "Even After All These Years," *Meg Vox Silver Linings, Mom Egg Review*, 2018; "The Paper Dolls of My Childhood" and "The Popular Girls in Seventh Grade," *Lips*, 2018; "I've Always Envied Women with Beautiful Hair," *San Diego Poetry Annual*, 2018; Frank Sinatra's Voice on the Jukebox," *Shrew Literary Review*, 2018; "So Many Things I Wish I Had Done," *Ragazine*, 2018; "Contemplating the Moon in My 77th Year," *The Night's Magician: Poems about the Moon*, 2018; "The Day After the Election," *Misrepresented People: Poetic Responses to Trump's America*, 2018; "Meatloaf and Hamburger Helper," *Crab Orchard Review*, 2018; "Taking My Brother to the Barber" and "Eighth Grade Kiss," *Lips*, 2019; "Ginestra and the Cotton Sheets," *Valley Voices*, 2019; "The Day the Sky Fell," *San Diego Poetry Annual*, 2019; "My Son the Lawyer Quotes Dylan Thomas to Give Me Courage," *Anthology on Aging*, 2019; "Ghost Voices," *Here: a poetry journal*, 2019; "I Can Still See My Mother," San Diego Poetry Annual, 2019; "Badge of Embarrassment," *Italian Americana*, 2019; "Cheap," *Prairie Schooner Portfolio*, Winter, 2019; "What Does the Child Inside Me Still Want," *Ovenbird*, 2020; "Carrying Their Hometowns to Paterson," The Face We Presented to the World," "In the Photograph, I am Sixteen," Today in The Workshop in Calabria, 2019," "This Morning on the Terrace," "Driving Through the Calabrian Landscape," "Approaching Morano," "Celebration in Albidona," *Celebrating Calbria! Writing Heritage and Memory*, Benedetto Publishers, Italy, 2020.

About the Author

Maria Mazziotti Gillan is a recipient of the 2014 George Garrett Award for Outstanding Community Service in Literature from AWP, the 2011 Barnes & Noble Writers for Writers Award from Poets & Writers, and the 2008 American Book Award for her book, *All That Lies Between Us* (Guernica Editions).

She is the founder /executive director of the Poetry Center at Passaic County Community College in Paterson, NJ, and editor of the *Paterson Literary Review*.

She is also a Bartle Professor and Professor Emerita of English and creative writing at Binghamton University-SUNY.

She has published twenty-three books. Her most recent books are the poetry and photography collaboration with Mark Hillringhouse, *Paterson Light and Shadow* (Serving House Books, 2017) and the poetry collection *What Blooms in Winter* (NYQ Books 2016.) Others include *The Girls in the Chartreuse Jackets* (Cat in the Sun Books, 2014); *Ancestors' Song* (Bordighera Press, 2013); *The Silence in an Empty House* (NYQ Books, 2013); *Writing Poetry to Save Your Life: How to Find the Courage to Tell Your Stories* (MiroLand, Guernica Editions, 2013); *The Place I Call Home* (NYQ Books, 2012); and *What We Pass On: Collected Poems 1980-2009* (Guernica Editions, 2010). She is co-editor of four anthologies with her daughter, Jennifer.

Visit her websites:
Poetry website: www.mariagillan.com
Poetry Blog: mariagillan.blogspot.com
New artist website: mariamazziottigillan.com

CPSIA information can be obtained
at www.ICGtesting.com
Printed in the USA
FSHW011459100321
79284FS